# Relics of Thought

Jeremiah Johnson

Presentation by *BookLeaf Publishing*

Web: www.bookleafpub.com

E-mail: info@bookleafpub.com

ISBN: 9789357744133

First edition 2023

# DEDICATION

I dedicate this book to yesterday's me. May this serve as proof of my creativity and a reminder that my goals can be achieved.

# ACKNOWLEDGEMENT

The first people I have to thank are my mum and dad. Thank you for supporting me; without both of you, there is no me.

Madi, thank you for your unwavering support.

Tom & Kobi thank you for feeding the fire that led to some of these; the WhatsApp poetry group was fun!

I also have to thank Book Leaf Publishing for the opportunity to provide a home for these poems.

Thank you to everyone else who has supported the creation of this in some way. It is truly appreciated.

# PREFACE

The title of this book plays on the idea that as we change, as society changes, the value we place on certain thoughts changes as well. Some thought processes perish while others are preserved. Sometimes the way we see the world decays over time due to trauma or hardship. My hope is that the book illustrates this in some way.

Each poem is the creative outcome of how I've interacted, empathised with, and processed the world around me. I hope some element of these resonates with you all.

This book came into being as part of the 21-day poetry challenge by Book Leaf Publishing. Prior to this challenge, many of these poems did not have a home. This challenge gave me the opportunity to sharpen my skills and organise my poems in a way that could be presented to you.

# Palpitations

I just need it all to stop!
My hand shakes
as the pain spreads from my back,
to my chest.
It's getting harder for my lungs to crack this
code,
A prickly feeling,
accompanies each breath.
Is it me,
or does the air seem thinner?
Each inhale feels like my last.
These gasps are audible,
I need to keep busy
I need to relax.
Deep breaths.
But there's no time.

My mind has entered a relay without my
permission.
Between hopelessness and restlessness the baton
change is seamless.
I can't keep up.
So like stiff calves I strain my memory to
remember,
that things aren't so bad.

But did I forget to tell you,
that I've forgotten how to breathe?
That my legs feel weak.

So much for muscle memory.
I can't even dance to my own tune.

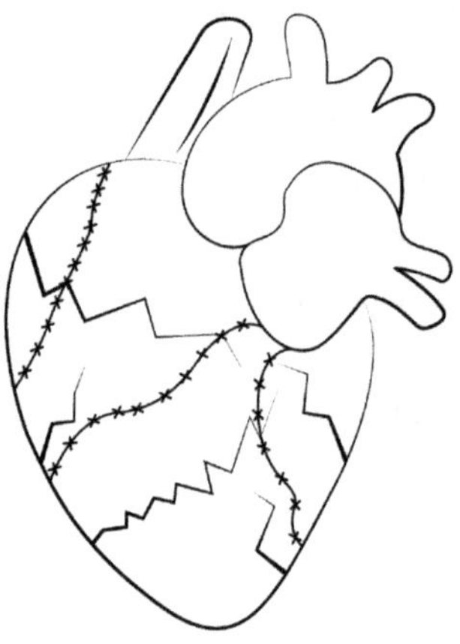

# Days On End....

The days have started to blur,
since dread
found the cure,
to its own displacement.
Nestled on the side
left uncovered
for lovers to slide into
my sanctuary,
is now a fortress.
I've spent sleepless nights
with my face pressed against the wall,
determined not to give in.
But who else can I confide in?
I'd grown tired of crying into my pillow,
waiting for something to save me.

That was my biggest mistake.

Waiting for something to save me.

The delusions of a lonely man.
I didn't know,
desperation could create companions,
that I'd come to depend on.
Ones that would convince me,
the floor was lava

and any attempts to act outside of my bed,
would burn me.
Failure was not an option
but lately,
resting between the bosoms of dread,
with the scent of burnt carpet filling my sinuses
finally, I realise
the tomorrow that I'd hoped for,
won't come.

# The Hum of Time

My body aches for the day,
that freedom
is more
than a fleeting dream,
whispered between iron bars
as we watch the stars
blink out
to make room for the sunrise.
A secret between them and you.
One you often wish you weren't so privy to.
Then the lonely
might seem less lonely,
and becoming a shadow of yourself
would be bearable.
Thoughts of better days
wouldn't turn into panic,
as darkness covers your eyes.

You relapse in silence.
Overwhelmed by the bright spark
of your past
and a future
where your potential is filled,
the burden of the present weighs heavy.
Both joys seem so far away.

Still,
the flicker of hope
drags your haggard body forward.
A dull sting
emanates from each step.

I wonder how many would resonate,
if I spoke about
the years I spent,
silencing my achievements
due to a fear of arrogance.
Inadvertently
giving birth to a pessimism
that now keeps me silent.
I tore at my skin
'til it became translucent.
Now your words can hurt me.
But my pride,
still has the power
to hide
those weak spots.
Sometimes it feels like
my Achilles heel
will kill me,
but in reality,
it won't.
Or it might,
it depends,
on my ability

to reframe circumstances
and conditions.
For example,
in your future
can you only see four walls
or can you see yourself being free?
Fuck the half empty
and the half full.
Can you see yourself being free
or not?
If not I get it.
The cage is a safe space,
you know each crevice
like the back of your hand.
The mice that reside
inside the walls,
have become
predictable companions.
You think that makes them trustworthy,
but it makes you
a fool,
for giving into
this false pretence
that loneliness
can be your new happiness,
and predictability
will fulfil you.

The road to riches
is never riskless.
Yet the biggest
risk you can take
is allowing time to flow through your fingers as
you remain still,
determined to wait the current out.
As if your ageing body
won't wither and break,
and by the time you realise
your mistake,
your dreams would have
already been lost.
Crushed
into sands of regret,
forever trapped
amongst the grains
of the Hourglass

# Enough!

How many more times can I write poems about
anxiety?
Or depression?
It's not like I don't have good things going for
me.
People who love me.
It's just,
it's just easier to write about how I've gone from
running from a black cloud,
to being swallowed by one.
And how the cloud holds my tears over my
head,
suffocating me with shame.
Besides,
the progressive nature of my regression deserves
to be documented.
Here is someone who gives all his light to the
world
at the expense of himself.
A grown man filled with so much suspense,
he neglects himself.

This is where,
I suppose I could tell you about self-care.
Let the poem make a turn for the better.
But that's something my self-esteem won't allow.

Better?
That's laughable.
There is no better,
when each corner of your mind
contains an excessive dose of morbidity.

# Distant Faith

As the weight on my chest
Threatens to swallow me
And there's nowhere else to turn
My sweaty palms find each other
As I turn to you.
I know I'm selfish,
A self-saboteur
Dependent on destructive behaviours.
And thought patterns
To soothe the pain.
I know
I've gained so many flaws
I'm not enough
Perhaps I never will be.
Standing on shaky legs as the floor sinks,
I'm not strong enough.

I've got so much more to say
This is the tip of the spiral
But I feel the embrace of your grace
Determined
To hold me
I'm reminded
That the only one,

Who knows me better than me
Is you.

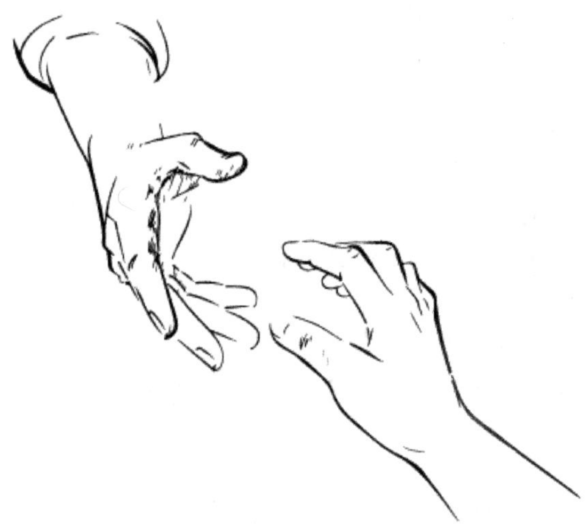

# Insanity of Silence (Part I)

Accusations of what you might be,
burn from the tips of their tongues like hot soup.
It was foolish to expect,
white privilege to swallow
a dish
full of home truths.
No matter how much you,
blow the meal before they eat,
the scotch bonnets give them red eyes.
With the heat surging through their senses,
they just can't believe you'd fix your lips,
to call them racist.
It's almost as though,
they're more disgusted with racism than you are.
They,
as in the one with the black friend.
The one with the eyes
that see the blue sky
but not the colour of my skin.
The one who uses the N-word because...
well rappers do.
Or maybe it's because we're "all human" and
that's a term of endearment.

Anyway....

Just like that
you're no longer the orator of your own story.
It's been colonised.
Each word a plantation
used to feed the narrative
that any act of microaggression,
or abuse,
comes from you.
You didn't even use the R-word.

You're trapped.
Swivelling on your desk chair,
between a rock and a hard place.
Insanity and integrity.

Am I mad?
You ask yourself,
as others inadvertently fuel your sense of
discomfort.
Their laughs sound like alarm bells.
But no-one else seems to hear it.
Your eyes find the exit.
You swallow the urge to flee.
Integrity.
You clench your fists to prevent yourself from
telling them to stop.
You work here.
You know the implications of integrity,

in a circle full of agents.
It's a war of attrition.

The art of silence,
often force-fed
through years of conflict and dismissal.
Starved of anything else,
it's become the food for survival.

# Airport Search (circa 2017)

Here we go again.
A man dressed in a uniform
invades my space,
and brings my autonomy down with
reassurances and excuses.
This won't take long
he says,
like our times taste the same.
As he conducts his quick search,
the Seconds,
Echo against my skin.
One hundred and eighty seconds
can seem like an awfully long time,
when you're being humiliated,
Pride mutilated
by the sorrowful stares,
the judgemental glances
from people,
who are relieved
not to be you.

Perhaps this is my fault,
this broken clock of a black body
should know what to expect in 2017.
But instead,

I'm frustrated,
because my sense of entitlement
is somehow
greater than what they think I deserve.

The airport search was done at random,
he says,
looking around
the similarities in skin colour must be a
coincidence then.
And I must be a king's fool
to fall
for such a foolish statement.
Sometimes you have to be honest
call a spade a spade,
admit, this system is racist as fuck.

But he has a job to keep.
I have a flight to catch.
So I hold my tongue.
And swallow the molten rock
before it can leak between my teeth.

Trap my rage!

Like a woman touched inappropriately in the
club,
while trying to make her way to the bar

Make a scene!

Be labelled an angry black woman or worse
if I make a scene,
I'll be labelled an angry black man and worse,

I don't care about labels,

I have a flight to catch.

So my tongue stays held
and I wear the silence on my face,
a cold,
unflinching stare.
They need to cower
under my gaze,
return my stolen power.
And as determined as they are
I do retrieve some,
Autonomy.
Only for them
to try and repeat the cycle
send me back
for another search,
but unfortunately for them,
my tongue,
can only be held,
for so long.

# Spotlight

Black lives matter.

The movement.

A moment.

The conscious act of existence and resistance
within a society
determined to justify
its own dehumanisation.
A window of opportunity,
for radical change.
But at what cost?
I guess that's selfish.
Or makes me lost
it's go hard or go home
but have you ever gone so hard for so long,
that every pushback
becomes a spasm,
sinking into your muscles
those fibres
forming chasms
as they're pulled apart.
Too many battles
from too many sides
you came in with enthusiasm.

Now you're jaded.
What's worse?
The violence of white silence,
or the performance of white outrage?
A race,
for centre stage
Black voices drowned out
as they take the mic.

Wait!!

Black voices should never be drowned out when
you take the mic.

Your ego.
Has taken the word Support,
and created the catchphrase
"I'll Save You".

Forcing yourself to become the protagonist in a
story
where you're not the main character
is just the recipe
for an entitled antagonist.
One who fails to see
the value in,
Autonomy

# The World Needs Saving

The world needs saving.
That's the conclusion he came to,
watching bodies fall
from tower windows,
like charred snowflakes.
Fire met Ice that night.
It's where he learnt
that not even flames filled with anguish
could melt the cold heart of austerity.
Several months on
the might of our cries
still meet with absolved responsibility.
Just typical,
for those in power to point fingers
everywhere
but at solutions and causes.
Going back and forth
telling us what we already knew,
like the Lammy review.

The world needs saving.
But can it be?
The doubt seeps into
his open wounds
as he lies face down,
already counting the seconds

until the next round.
He was flogged,
for being Black.
In an African country no less.
Why are black bodies
always seen as the main fodder
for barbarians?
Is it because their power
comes from our blood?

The world needs saving.
She's not the one to save it though.
Not when
the world holds a knife to her throat.
She use to wonder
when sexism
would be acknowledged like racism,
until she noticed that
racism wasn't being acknowledged either.
So here she sits,
in the overlap of confinements,
a margin
within a margin.
There's never been enough space
for her to tell her story,
even within this poem.

The world needs saving.
I cannot save it.
Not with this crippling fear
of failure.
It takes a steel spine
to shoulder
some of earth's burdens.
Mine has withered.
Or at least
it feels that way.
Despite the struggle to stand straight,
my passion
is my crutch,
pushing me forward
in spite of myself.
Although,
when I look at me
it's hard to see
much else but anxiety.
I also see
Him,
And Her,
And Them.
I see a Black body
dancing on the periphery of cages
designed to confine their greatness.
I see a body
burnt beyond recognition,
name lost,

justice still to be served.

The world needs saving.
And I cannot save it.
Perhaps none of us can.

# Insanity of Silence (Part II)

Perhaps this humanity thing is overrated.
Because with privilege,
comes the ability,
to position yourself at the centre of any human
experience.
Turning the tables on the oppressed,
painting them as oppressors.
Where any harm you've caused,
becomes their "agenda",
designed to
forever warp the fabric of your identity.
Turning you,
or God forbid,
your children,
into creatures of the night.
Black and brown gay disabled bodies
walk among us,
waiting for the wake of the moon
to strike,
with fangs filled with
representation and acceptance.
Their marginalisation
is something to be feared,
dare you,
jump over the fence and mix,
you'll never be human again.

Now their attempt at integration??!!

Is to be met with two silver bullets.
Try to be equal at your own risk.

I wonder if I have survivor's guilt.
Does the black in me survive the onslaught
because of my sexuality?
Tired and wounded
I can seek healing amongst those that share my
hue,
the second bullet cannot hurt me,
so I don't need to think about it.

Still, my friends play Russian roulette
unaware that language can be oppressive and
kill.
Or maybe they're not.
Maybe my guilt,
has woven a delusion
for them to snuggle into.

I'm a glutton for comfort,
I choose isolation over confrontation
and convince myself that the silence
equates to progress.

The truth is,
silence is a slow burn
to the matchsticks of my sanity.
The question of whether
your friends would be your friends
if you were gay,
seeps into the crevices of my thoughts.
Doubt is a sad realisation.

Perhaps this humanity thing is overrated.
Selective at best.
Non-existent at worse.
I have the luxury of flitting between the two,
this black,
straight body
with an invisible cloak over its,
disability.

# Uneven Ceiling

This uneven ceiling.
A shelter,
for cherished memories
of a childhood
where innocence met fun
Christmases,
spent christening new games.
It's hard to ask for more.
When these brick and plastered walls,
held me at my highest.
Nestled tightly on the top bunk,
sleepovers were a dream.
4 man,
head to toe.
Birthdays were a dream.
Those days
all I needed was a PlayStation
and space
To beat friends
A permanent station
To rest
Without a weapon under my pillow.

Instead
under my pillow sat books.
And eventually journals.
Gratitudes and affirmations
replaced Percy Jackson
when fantasy
was no longer enough
to distract from the anxiety.

Home had its moments.

But I've always come back.

Perhaps I've outgrown its safety.
And though dependence
can become a hindrance,
the smell of nostalgia holds me.
Like a mother's beak,
latched to her baby's wing.

# Spirit Unborn

Although we haven't met
face to face,
remember that we reside
in the same place.
Your body
acting as my duvet,
protecting me
from the boogeyman.
An adamantium shield.
Unbreakable.
Almost.
You see,
there was a chink in our armour
that you just couldn't see.
But he did.
Ironic that
the one who was meant to,
protect you,
hurt you.
Tearing a hole through time,
a time
where we would have met.
And I
would have become whole,
laughing every morning
as you tickled me awake,

birthdays sail by
and with every cake,
my wish remains the same.
For your smile to never fade.

But circumstances may have made
your smile fade
forever.
To be replaced with a frown,
etched to your face
like the tattoo of my name on your wrist.

I'm sorry.

I'm sorry that my absence
has left you hollow.
My demise,
is a hard pill to swallow
so I don't blame you
if you wish you had swallowed
one earlier.
Back before,
my heart beat in tune to yours,
creating melodies for the pores,
giving you that summertime glow.
So thank you,
because without you
there could be no me.
And I will always be with you.

So don't cry mummy
don't cry.
For me mummy,
live happy.
So when we meet at first, it will be
with smiles that never fade.

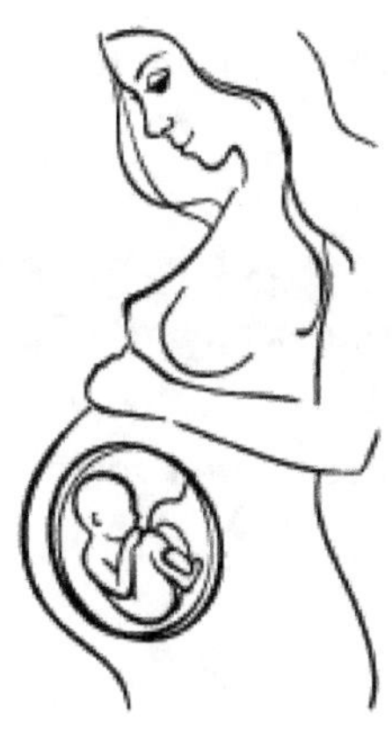

# A Quick Word With X
## (R.I.P)

At 50,
you told us that you had found peace.
As I tiptoe towards 30,
I wonder,
if I'll have to wait that long
for my peace
to find its way home.
If we can't have our cake and eat it,
does that mean addicts,
will spend lifetimes chasing peace
just because their escape route differs slightly?

Tell me,
when your son spoke of the pressures he faced,
trying to meet your standards of masculinity,
did it crush you?
Or did his softness remind you of your own
heart?

I've seen smiles freeze over
as boys learn what it takes to be men.
Youthful innocence exploited by olders
masquerading as mentors.

Was this betrayal a source of your own anger?
Or your generosity?
Because you didn't choose to be,
burdened with demons
Yet somehow they made an angel out of you.

# Surface Smiles

At first glance
The image is picture perfect,
Black tie
Tied neatly around a fresh shirt
The colour of summer clouds.
You walk with a smile so bright
It reflects on the faces of others.
Contagious,
Like a baby's laugh
Your innocence,
Fills me with envy.
How,
Can you exist in a world so ugly?
I'm not sure
If that question is for you,
Or me.
Am I projecting my trepidations
Like a black dad
Warning his black son
About those blue lights
But sometimes,
When I squint hard enough,
I can make out the bruises
Beneath your collared shirt.
So tell me,

If you roll up your sleeves
Will I find scriptures carved
Across your arms
In permanent ink?
Does your jagged heart
Press against your lung,
When you try to breathe?
Beneath the aesthetics
You're hurting,
Yet you shoulder everyone's bliss

# How Does It Feel To Be A Weapon?

Our bodies press tightly against each other
Is it greed
That feeds this carnal desire?
Your groans shudder through me
As I stifle my own,
Determined to devour you.

I've found solace
Within the folds of your wetness
Still I push further
Grateful, for the strength bestowed upon me.

Deeper, I go
To a place
Where pleasure dulls every sense.

The scream that I cannot hear, dies in your
throat.
The hands holding me tightly, fall limp.
I retract
Almost lost to the bliss of it all
Your metallic taste anchors me.
I have devoured you.
Perhaps one day

I too shall be devoured.
This sharp-edged body, melted down
Moulded,
For a different purpose.

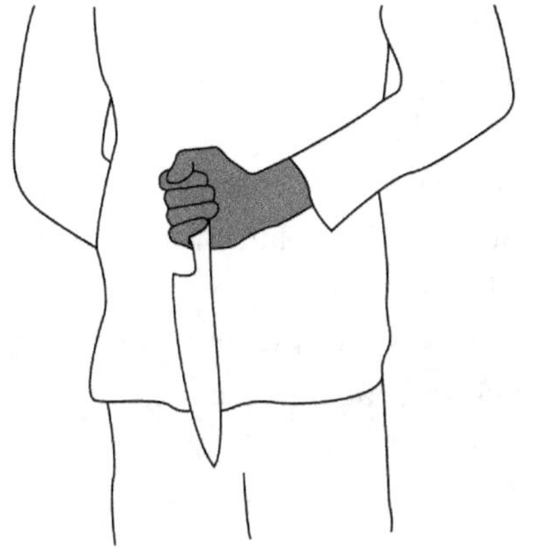

# Wine

My form is quiet
Disarming,
I settle neatly into a handsome bottle
Waiting for my turn.
My belly churns in acknowledgment
That my turn will come.
It always does.
This world is too troublesome
For me not to be needed
I am a reprieve
A lens through which things can look better.
At times I feel nothing,
This is why I am worn with such fervour,
My skin protects against the cold.

# Snowflake

The soft shackles release me.
As I slowly descend
The relief of being free
Turns into trepidation
I feel the sun's anger against my skin
It does not want me here
Still,
The cold air pushes me on...
Towards smiling faces.
Arms outstretched,
I settle.
As a gloved finger traces
The outline of where I once was.

# Bottle to Water

As I behold your shapeless form,
and admire the beauty of transparency
it dawns on me,
to hold and protect something so pure,
is the greatest honour.

You are burdened with great expectations.
They recognise the good you do.
And exploit it.
Contain you
using other versions of me.
Different faces
with a different price.
Being of service shouldn't come at a cost
to those you are meaning to serve.

You taught me that.

Sometimes,
I catch the sorrow in your shimmer.
You are a miracle.
I've seen you wash away sickness.
Yet you are often overlooked.
Or worse.
Forced to mix with those that only wish to harm.

www.ingramcontent.com/pod-product-compliance
Lightning Source LLC
LaVergne TN
LVHW051231200726
843510LV00011B/1552